Somebody Else Sold the World

Somebody Else
Sold the World

ADRIAN MATEJKA

PENGUIN POETS

PENGUIN BOOKS

An imprint of Penguin Random House LLC
penguinrandomhouse.com

LIBRARY OF CONGRESS CATALOGING-IN-PUBLICATION DATA
Names: Matejka, Adrian, 1971– author.
Title: Somebody else sold the world / Adrian Matejka.
Description: [New York] : Penguin Books, [2021] | Series: Penguin poets |
Identifiers: LCCN 2021001327 (print) | LCCN 2021001328 (ebook) | ISBN
9780143136446 (paperback) | ISBN 9780525507987 (ebook)
Subjects: LCGFT: Poetry.
Classification: LCC PS3613.A825 S66 2021 (print) | LCC PS3613.A825
(ebook) | DDC 811/.6—dc23
LC record available at https://lccn.loc.gov/2021001327
LC ebook record available at https://lccn.loc.gov/2021001328

Printed in the United States of America

1st Printing

Set in Cochin LT Std
Designed by Catherine Leonardo

For Jon and Pops

CONTENTS

Sung Entropy

Different Violences

& My Heart Beside

Charcoal Underbone

Antagonists All Over

It's all I have to bring today—
This, and my heart beside—
—EMILY DICKINSON

You're face to face
with the man who sold the world.
—DAVID BOWIE

Sung Entropy

SOMEBODY ELSE SOLD THE WORLD

& before I knew it, the violet sky
flagged with the sun's violent
demands: for magnolias in bloom,
natural light, any place magnanimous
without locks or doors. Different
kinds of masks for being & breathing.
The antagonists with their vanity tans
& usual mischiefs whistled jingles
about liberties & wars as we buttoned
up our confinement & dreamed about
hugging. We talked about *was* & *when*
when we missed our friends & dentist
appointments. Molars dropped out
without breathable air. Hair forgot
its natural colors without testimonies
at intersections & barbeques. Words
lost their family recipes. Friends lost
their words, then lost their parents.
A masked few found love somehow
in the gerrymandered grocery lines
& farmers' fields upturned with unsellable
vegetables. So the antagonists cornered
the curfews, manufacturing arguments
with guns at the ready like henchmen.
The air around us was so ripe, it might
have broken in half if we could touch it.

ON THE B SIDE

The song ends because the beginning
doesn't jump-start again: red smudge

of a mouth, lipstick all over the place
like the afterthought a comet leaves

on its way out. What makes this moment
unfold like a woman raising herself

up from an unfamiliar couch? Honky-
tonk in the blue honey of an eyeball?

Perfume & its circus of heart-shaped
introductions? Innuendo always

stumbles in the lead-in, like a man
pawing around for his busted spectacles

after waking up in the world's stubble.
Hand over hand he paws, through

guitar picks & record changers, busted
gut strings & clothing strung with

familiar vibrato outside the window.
He could be Bowie himself, exhausted

by skyscrapers cracked in the aftermath
of a smile. His eyes aren't different

colors. They just have different focuses.
He could be a whole lot of nothing:

thinning hair, low change in his right
pocket jingling down the stairs.

He was given all of it & stole the best
of the rest. Even without glasses,

he sees her nearly dressed: 33 ⅓ rpm
stacticky in the lead-out's harmony.

IT WAS OVER WAY BACK THEN

because of want & tumble?
Because of word crumbles

in the kitchen's halogen?
No. Separate bedrooms

for years & here I am again:
up top in the kitchen light,

out front with a burnished
stove & the microwave's

immaculate readouts. Up
here, my crosscut hands

greet the butter knife before
the big spread. What I want

now is a better ideogram
for *instead* after the skull

& crossbones on the pill bottles.
What I want is a bucket for

my panics & justifications.
My coddled addendums

downtagged on the sales table
each & every spring. Here

we go with that old seasonal
bullshit again. Earphones on

so your eardrums don't get
punched out near the exit.

Tom Fords on, too, just
for the flex of it. Is it

too much to ask for quiet
after all my losses in this

insistent chorus of renew?
Is it too much to be momentary

in the morning grass, suede
kicks beaten up by the dew?

HAUL

I used to live in a sandstone house
wrapped up in flowers. They weren't
tall like Neruda's in his city next

to the sea. My flowers quickstepped
like the town I walked the dog
through—little magentas, roses,

singsong rehearsals of sing-along
yellows & winking whites when
the right breeze kicked up. Out

in the yard, neighborly blossoms
falsettoed to the canopy each & every
spring. Suburb of aromatic layers,

trimmed hedges pollenating the windows
while my little girl gospeled down
the long stair of revelry. Glory be.

Her harmony bent me like a stark
song in the back talk. Euphonium
along the length of yawning houses,

those For Sale signs & empty
windows with timed lights. Every
thing sang its entropy. Almost

everybody grew eventually. Not by
revolution but realization: nostalgia
made mnemonic. What else could

I do after leaving that house other
than become part of the chorus?
Glory be my aberrant attendance,

still trying to itemize the litany
of sunstruck days the way
Sisyphus did, hauling his bundled

shipwreck up to the recycler
for a few copper coins & a smoke.
Glory be my busted, fatherly heart.

GYMNOPÉDIES NO. 1

That was the week it wouldn't stop
snowing. That was the week five-
fingered trees fell on houses & power
lines snapped like somebody waiting
for payday in a snowstorm. That snow
week, my little girl & I trudged over
the busted branches fidgeting through
the snow like empty digits through
a hungry pocket. Over the termite-
hollowed stump, squat as a flat tire,
then up & over the hollow the fox dives
into when we open the back door.
That week glittered like a Christmas
card while we poked around for
the best place to stand a snowman.
A pinecone-nosed one. One with
thumb-pressed eyes to see the whole
picture once things warm up.

HEARING DAMAGE

I had a trumpet shaped
like a downward heart
& I played it recklessly.

All of its dented iterations
of brass & bell. Three-
valve marginality.

Marching band possibility
pointing at the muddy
dirt. I had a double-talk

as slick & overachieving
as a kid trench-coated
with a boom box overhead

in the rain. His socks:
wet & ankle loose
in their blueness.

Argyle wonder caught
up in high school's sloppy
gears, greedy for moments

of matriculated attention.
& none of it worked—
when the tape deck got

soaked, the tape stopped
playing. When the music
stopped, her shades

barked when they shut.
As if attention itself
magnetized, stretched

around eager reels, then
fed itself into the machine.
Click, click, click.

As if my bleating pleas
weren't big trumpets
for attention, but gentle

half notes trimmed into
funny polyester hearts,
future palpitations of glory.

SOMEBODY ELSE SOLD THE WORLD

So much yellow gold
on me like a beehive

—FUTURE

Everything goes better with gold
for the antagonists. They gild teeth
& toilet caps with it. They write
grocery lists & postscripts with it
while the rest of us cluster around
the jewelry shop hoping we'll catch
a sale before it's Valentine's Day
again. Old traditions of huddling
against the elements learned
back in the butt-naked day, mewling
at the sky's conditions. I'm jewelryless
& archaic, sure, still calling love
by its twentieth-century name.
I'm abiding by the general rituals
while making all the wrong choices
right next to a case full of pendants
blinking like my future paramour's
eyes. I'm still looking upward, sure,
prayer hands folded on top of the leather
hymnal. Every one of my busted loves
chaptered & bound with gold leaf
& not even the stars that gold comes
from could save my copper-plated
routines. Future called it *astronaut status,*

ATL skyline glamorous behind him.
Some astronauts' smiles look like
golden cityscapes. Some astronauts
have gold wings & wedding rings,
too, cast from the first available cluster.

LOVE NOTES

Do you love vague commitments?
Do you love bad news in crooning shapes?
Whole or half, tattoos mooning on

conjoined rib cages? Check this box &,
like a breath, you'll feel mostly bygone.

Like one of those early recordings, you'll
be scratchy & demystified. Untranscribably
confessional until the last quarter note

is a processional. You'll be absolutely fine,
flipped to the B side of this note's high-lined

referendum. Magnificent & stark inside
the addendum, like a big breath exhaled
through the smart part of a question mark.

HIGHEST

I'm the highest in the room

—TRAVIS SCOTT

I rise up, therefore I must be like Descartes
if he didn't finish all the reading. I raise up

like the highest Black hand in history class.
I am risen like the blood pressure of anybody

Black mimeographed in the chronic textbook
of this monochromatic year. That's infant

mortality rate high. That's high-top fade high.
Most everything up here hangs threadbare,

squarely in the redline of summery excuses.
Everything else up in here, from the cop

apologies to the solidarity statements: a double
tap of distraction for somebody else's

high sign. That's unemployment high. That's
Machu Picchu high. What a relief hardly

anybody stuck around to see me on the low
side of the mountain. What a reprieve because

I kept rising stealthily—past my historical
anxiety, way past all my inherited hearsay

until I am so high up on the shelf I eye-
level alchemy. Even up here, I'm adept

at shrinking myself for safety. Even up here,
my shoulders hunch like a small analogy.

Different Violences

SOMEBODY ELSE SOLD THE WORLD

Hunger is an antagonist.

—BEN OKRI

Outside, the antagonists
are wet with flag colors
& sycophancy & I'm alone

in the front room again
like it's 1982 again when
the power got cut off

& the neighbors brawled
like sullen countries over
the demarcation of kitchen

table & china hutch. Another
revolution breaking in half,
another slim-ringed alliance

snapped under the weight
of lost referendums. Where did
their long-stemmed love go?

Even now, I'm sitting in
the window seat in the year
of cottonmouth & disaffection

as white people goose-step
masklessly & the antagonists
imagine new ways to dismantle

poor people. Sitting, running,
dreaming, coughing, seeming:
cuffs for all of them. Bullets,

too, glinting in perpetual
velocity. To be poor is to always
be blamed for your already

busted happenstance. There's
no changing that American
tradition now, not even during

a pandemic. Meanwhile,
the antagonists boat out
to their islands of isolation

& repose. Anything they need
is essential, while the rest of us
stay in place like furniture.

BULLET PARTS

Primer (Brass + Lead)

The bullet base is made from the kind of brass that otherwise
would have been a classroom doorknob or cheap ring at one
of those prequarantine gathering spots with games of chance
& lights that surprise & delight. Or molded into new French
horns for the underfunded youth band—no solos for the hornists,
but they are still vital to the orchestra. At the center of the brass
base: an igniter made out of lead. An igniter is only good
at exploding, but the lead might have scratched love in meticulous
notes with old-time penmanship. Or become part of the paint
behind a periodic table of elements in the back of a public school
classroom: Pb, atomic number 82. It's right there, lining Roman
aqueducts & wine vats at the other end of the empire. It's right
there, holding reactors & their radiations close as a friend in need.
Walkman batteries running out in the middle of a slow jam again—
the voices get thicker & deeper in the tape correction. In some other
life, the primer probably would have gone in another direction.

Rim (Brass)

Big-brimmed accomplice,
castoff of copper & zinc.
Ballistic of tough talk

& easy pickup. You might
have been the lower lip
of a brass mouth that never

learned its own etiquette.
Still crimped, still pinched:
you could have been alloyed

as a rib for caging some
other, amended fauna
in the arboretum of murderers

where out-of-season hunters
line up for hours just
to ogle your affable flange.

Propellant (Gunpowder or Cordite)

Gunpowder, like poetry,
was mistaken for an immortality

potion. Poetry, like gunpowder,
was first used to light up

the sky with every color outside
a summer window. AD 700,

& the first propellant welcomed
the new year with combustible

surprise & eye-covering brightness.
Gunpowder: easily misunderstood

as medicine in its beauty, raising
dragons & open-palmed stars bird-

level in the sky, while cordite can't
be anything other than the killer

it was mixed to be. Since 1889,
nitrocellulose, nitroglycerine,

& petroleum jelly—a murderous
clique. Cordite is only good at killing.

Since 1889, cordite has made killing
easier for the bright-badged killers.

Case (Brass or Steel)

Brass again, wishing to be a lost key or a better Victorian decoration. Brass again, wanting to be badged in a gentle fashion. Steel, too, taken from the sides of ships or the skeletons of skyscrapers. Steel can be a fist-bumped architecture, full of the empty seats fans used to sit in. Or car bumpers dented in claustrophobia. The stop sign nobody slows down for when cops aren't around at the fork in the road. Forks in the drawers of the local establishments that only serve takeout now & butter knives for the drunken disagreements, past & future. Nerves steeled by food & beer. Abs of steel, too, in the old commercials on the TV in the corner.

Bullet (Lead + Alloy)

Lead in the belly, copper
& nickel skin in abundance
each year. Ten billion bullets
made in America each year.
Enough bullets to kill all
of the earth each year.
The bullet hits three times
faster than we can hear
its concussion. The bullet
breaks the air with its 2,182
mph admission. The bullet
is a grim onomatopoeia
for itself. The bullet is
a slim allegory for a gun-
happy nation & its attendant
segregations. Lead belly,
wrapped in the grinning
freedom amendment: a gun
is almost more important
than what comes out of it.
A gun is always more
important than the people
in front of it. Here we are
again: so many Black women
& Black men in front of it.

SOMEBODY ELSE SOLD THE WORLD

I don't know if I should excuses
It's a really good deal excuses
It's not mine even if I could excuses
If I don't do it someone else would excuses
If I don't play along I'll be excuses
I'm committed to it now see excuses
Oh no not me excuses
Excuse me I'll get you back next Tuesday
Let us go you & I excuses
Excuse me because I loved you too much
Excuse me because I swerved too much
Well what had happened after it was excuses
Well I planned to catch a bus after it excuses
It was dark & he was dark recuse me
There was no one to help me excuses
I was worried about my safety excuses
What about me excuses
Excuse me what about me

TUESDAY FEELING

*Take it or leave it
it's what you're owed*
— BLOOD ORANGE

Slowest-footed day of the week,
wrong-noted & creaking on
the credenza while the other

influencers gossip in the kitchen's
linoleum. Weekend rebound:
no football on the tube, no football

anywhere—not even the touch
kind in your parents' backyard,
white trellises flowering where

the sidelines could be. Tuesday,
you're built out of absolution,
then named after a war god

during a forgotten armistice. Day
of lipstick battles, day of burger
repayments & corn-chip salads

in cafeterias all over Indiana.
Tuesday, you remind me
of something I can't remember.

Droll day when even reruns regret
rerunning on you. Basic day
when nothing succeeds except

spiked elections & obligatory
divorce school way out in Beech
Grove or Zionsville. It's all because

of you: big day of paper ballots,
big day of metal detectors
& powdered coffee creamer

in the distrustful cups of exes.
Meanwhile, most of us misfits
sit in foldout chairs pretending

to scroll our phones during
your prime hours. Just like
the others, I've been wishing for

better epiphanies. Just like
you, I've been pretending I was
a different day most of my life.

WAKE UP, YOUNG LOVERS

You've already confessed your bone-spun dictums to almost
every bohemian with ears. You've held hands all up & down
the lovers' lanes & even mashed up your pet names. Look
at you: hearts for eyes, thumpers for brains—luxury of two
as a little moon clips like a corsage onto the night's lapel just
for you. You've watched each other sleep in the full-throated blue.
Behind the edge of you, bricks go through windows & bullets
go through people. This variegated world is your aphorism while
bodies are broken apart irreparably & buildings simmer & burn.

& My Heart Beside

IT'S ALL I HAVE / DAYDREAMING

I once got so high, I couldn't
remember if I loved me as much
as I loved you. My mezzanined
thin dream. My slipstreamed
wish list. My knees wobble
like the octaves above the sun
clocks when you look at me.
& the bees, the bees: phosphenes
swirling at five o'clock every day.
I once got so hyped, the buzzing
sounds cleared out my ears while
previous Christmases piled into
questions. They reopened infatuations
as almost reality. They broke
my reservoir of debt eventually.
In the damage, even imaginary
oceans need imagined plankton
& so I ended up in the boathouse
of quotations. Sometimes bees
seem sentimental as they fan
the air with things I don't feel
like talking about: my old life,
Pops, Jon. What else could I do
after letting go other than
hum at the water? All this loss,
mystifying as hydrology. None
of it relieves my dreams
of the three of us in Seattle by

the glittering lake. It's backdropped
by mountains as the water recedes.
The turtles here submerge when
geometrically convenient. Fish,
too, finning in temporary current.
All of us backstroking, so there's
only sky to see clearly in the soak.

SOMEBODY ELSE SOLD THE WORLD

& by now even the unemployed
cat burglars appreciate sunrises
for their reliability. Nobody
knows how to act when days
of shelter-in-place are insistent
as my middle-aged backache
& minutes bend back into inelastic
middles. Nothing to do in this
daylessness except listen to music
I've already heard. Kurt Cobain said
Spring is here again, but it's already
been May for months. I miss friends,
even the ones I don't really like.
The ones who move with the same
malaise as these do-over days,
hollow as trumpets. Meanwhile,
the man who sold the world, then
skipped town, is bewildered under
his amnesiac sky. From his vantage,
the whole thing is combed over
with victorious clouds. But really,
it's just truck exhaust streamered
over the unmasked faces below
his balcony of belief. Up & down
don't mean a thing when you have
everything. That's why he moves
selfishly like his timepieces do—
circuitous & automatic: tick, tick.

LET'S GET ACQUAINTED

while we talk about hunger & loss. I once had artful chatter
    before it got
unsustainable. I once pumped everything around me like an
    unrelatable
heart. Once I spaced out at the skull-bright codicil before it
    got bland
& unreliable. I once had a red hammer in my hand. I played it
    in the freight car
of my singing emancipation. I once had, I once had. Two
    guitars from
the pawnshop instead of feet & I still couldn't swing my big
    ideas. A woman so fine
I quit eating meat of any style. I once had sixteenth notes
    where other people have gears.
An altruistic jones for affection & touching despite my
    engineering. So much
I didn't matter as much. I once had a heart but sold it for
    sauce. I once had
some semi-glossed gators but lost them in the static. Really: I
    had a double
cross & a six-string, clean as tap water. I lost both beauties in
    the radiator
steam. Really, I had somebody who loved my frets & strings
    forever.
Imagine that: anybody loving my rust-bucket & cardiac needs
    together.

GYMNOPÉDIES NO. 2

In NYC, we stalked fishes
in filets of sounds. This was
the before days: delivery
engines & ashy doors clapping
shut, vendors knuckling fin-
& silhouette-shaped words
into salty expectations. Not
a double-ply mask anywhere.
We walked down a couple
slim-bricked blocks that smelled
like snapper & afro sheen
with no afros in sight.
On snaggletoothed streets,
we double-took the wet
alleys where things jumped
off the hook like smart seafood
before lunch. We parted
the perfect & abundantly
wintered streets right before
my little girl said *I know*
all these parts like a tired
pianist resting on her bench.

IT'S JUST A GUESS

so the record diminuendos
on its own & the old notes
in the lead-out seem
less summery. The latch
relatching its familiar up
& in as the LP stops.
It's easy to overlook
the arm returning since
it doesn't have any place
else to go. Local spiders
corner their satisfactions
& the hallway is less lavender,
fewer love notes bleating
in the wind ensemble.
Nobody talks about
adolescence's actual smell
in the preamble. One
weekday you're sniffling
in a food court way up
on the north side, ordering
a crummy slice & a pop
while the teenage version
of you behind the counter
checks sexts on a greasy
phone. "Let's Stay Together"
is playing & the kid doesn't
know any of the words.

The next: you're slow-
dancing inside another
country's consonants
as its mountains stand
back in an unpronounceable
stack. Somewhere between,
the record begins its wet
yesterdays again. I guess
I'm doing fine, I say whispery
as static behind the door
I'm still closing. All nine
volts in the vocal cords went
out again, so there's not
a lot to say while music
circles this way. Maybe
love is more vernacular
than secular anyway.

GYMNOPÉDIES NO. 3

This sunlight on snow. This decrescendo
of covered stumps & brush—stop for it. Stop
before the sled end-over-ends down the chin

of the hill—the way it always will at the rock
⅔ of the way down. Stop & shiver in it: ring

of snow inside gloves, cusp of red forehead under
the hat like a sun just waiting to top the hill. Every
ill-built snowball waiting to be thrown, every

bell-shaped angel stamped into the brown leaves.
Back before, when my little girl ranged in winter,

she rearranged its dazzling veneer—crestfallen
pinecones, grizzled beards of bushes in the morning,
furnace's windup huffing a throat-clearing of snow.

LOVE NOTES

Do you love the way we sound off in the wheelhouse?
Us in a brainpan party, circumnavigating the double-
talk on heels made out of feathers? The sky is right there,

closer to the sun than our upward etiquette. Yes. No.
On the incandescent dais of embarrassment, did you

check both ways to see if the stiletto got bent? Did you
check into the hotel of strong choices? This is the big eclipse
remixed as melody: harmonic, egalitarian, until eighth notes

give up their facade & beaks & necks show themselves
to be breaks & wrecks. All the familiar faces: they flap

upside down, cheeping the habitual tunes. They're dull
as Monday morning. Sometimes love is mundane that
way. Other times it spins as gently as Icarus's night-light.

IT'S IMPOSSIBLE TO BREATHE TREES

The whole snowy carapace rustles
as trees bend in needful poses
& the knuckled trucks pass below

them again, road salt crunching
like all of the wishful thinking
that we'd be past this virus by now.

& we can all be thankful that mittened
hands & knitted hats & lingering
Christmases with real presents

under pretend trees are precursors
to some kind of thick thaw in the next
couple of months. All of the buds

will crack open at the first unsealing
of somebody's winterized windows.
The piano music the windows used

to muffle will key easily in the open
air. Residual cough of rabbits, then
a stretch of birds—little victories

in the sky. Buttercup blossoms
breaking at shoe height & the little
girl of my memory, long gone now:

constant swirl of splendor. It will be
good to run through the tight curls
of bees as the trees share their ideas

just beneath us. It will be good
to watch things spin effortlessly,
as if we weren't even here.

Charcoal Underbone

SOMEBODY ELSE SOLD THE WORLD

& later, the first round
of conscriptions in the parking

lot of Eli Lilly's headquarters
crescendos like background

singers over the long street
of birds. In the synchronization

of handmade masks & distance,
the possibly contaminated

air moves like the cognate
of a person: it has walking

shoes as scuffed as a music
conductor's. Its hands, needy

as a politician's. The whole
neighborhood pops with

unknowing while optimistic
birds chirp & skip & chirp

from left to right along black
power lines that fuel the normal

human noise that's quiet now.
Ambulance sirens lift above

the car engines idling in testing
lines. Those climate-controlled

sedans & pickups, windows
tight like the caution-vested

testers' faces directing them
to one lane or another. Iridescent

cones split the street into typical
halves of haves & have-nots.

I SAY THE THING FOR THE FIRST TIME

& what comes after? Charcoal
underbone, some darkroom

for soliloquy & irises wide
at home. Some other glitter

party popping off & ending
with me counting resignations

on a couch made out of my last
pennies. Copper profiles lost

in the cushions dull with
emancipation & worth almost

me. Button nicks instead
of eyes. Green patina instead

of skin over presidential profiles.
How to separate the awkward

exhales from full-body anxieties?
The song in the park across

the street bumps something
about love & flowers, but I can't

split my requiem from its simple
leather. Sneakers arrhythmically

skeletal, squeaking left, then right,
in somebody else's want garden,

midtown in a cracked city
split by a river so cluttered with

rough history, it's eye level
to the flustered blackbirds.

SNAKES BECAUSE WE SAY SO

—for daughters everywhere

Redheaded boys are snakes.
Blonde boys are snakes.
Those brunette boys with
their shaggy, dreamy hair—
them, too. Snakes, all of them:
out in the yard, cartwheeling
into last-of-summer purple
just to impress. Freewheeling
with synth soundtracks, chests
puffed to impress. Snakes
are naturally inflated that way.
Whichever antagonist yelled
"snake" in the game-day
bleachers has snake-like manners.
In the standard light of weekday
pews, snakes are Baptist guilt
minus legs. Empty baptism
rivers are snakes. Empty dance
floors are snakes. Most snakes
are guilty because we need
to blame somebody. Most boys
fight so much because we
can't tell anybody. Some
body is a snake in a human
hat. Some human in a red

hat snakes his way past
the abandoned garden while
asking all the wrong questions.
Snakes didn't ask for any
of this. Snakes wanted to be
a boy with opposable thumbs,
but woke up one May with
a shoulderless heart skipping
beneath new, malleable skin.

COUNT TO FIVE

I'm all out of place
—RHYE

I shouldn't even be out,
squeezing into these melodic
habits as the afternoon
gets overcast & models-
in-waiting return snappable
heels, sunglasses on the tops
of their sun-kissed heads.
Everyone is masked
& somehow stays
beautiful in their buoyant
mantras. Nobody panics
except me. Nobody feels
out of place except me.
The hangers-on hit
the mini-mart for menthols
& juice. Everybody
but me with someplace
to be & I'm not supposed
to be here, middle-aged
as medieval script
on a silk shirtsleeve.
Things have changed
since the last time I was
outside the outdoor mall
on somebody else's

street of pet sounds.
I'm just trying to keep dust
out of my crow's-feet.
My front jeans pockets:
abundant with outmoded
dad things, but I'm
still feeling myself in
the tradition of dads.
Grand flex of self-
delusion at two o'clock,
the clock's non sequitur.
A time that's a little
stretched out like me,
uncertain in its assurances.
Just because I know
you're the one for me
doesn't mean I'm one
of the ones for you.
Just because love
is correlative doesn't
mean I understand
masked interrogatives.

LOVE NOTES

Come through my lit, incantatory touch.
Come through my resplendent crush: even
the breeze seems like a huff of basic

aromatics when you swirl into the banter.
Come into the handwritten rhapsody where

my heart remains an unusual pronunciation.
The trees flutter with pretend breath.
The birds therein are mostly lazy & handsy.

I can't see them, but from the heart way out
to the trees: mitral humility. As in *Yes,*

please to whatever your requests may be.
Your questions became this note in cursive.
This note is the memory of trees just like us.

HARMONY IS MOSTLY REVOLUTIONARY

& now everybody is some kind
of delicious fetish. A whole
chorus of proclivities, full-throttled
in the washbowl of next-door
freaky: those Picasso lickable
toes ones. Candle wax on skin
for some. Those forehead-camera
recording ones. Wigs are optional
on some of them. The *it happens
to a lot of guys*, sitting on the edge
of the bed just like a rerun.
The suctioned toys on the wall
for solo fun & the *Yes, whatever*
& then somes. Meanwhile,
another antagonist wobbles by
the conjunction of satisfaction
on a busted heel. With that rip
in her stocking, she's as oblivious
as a cloud in the early evening.
So thick in her own arbitered
heart she can't hear the tassels
swishing or the cuffs clinking.

COINCIDENCE/ACCIDENT

Here we are, all up
in the luminosity
of my lucky, lit morning.

From sealess Indy
to that bit-clean ocean
where blues contagiously

move contiguously
upside down. Here we
are. From the churlish

river to the brown curls
of Paris humidity:
I've been waiting for

this my whole solo
career. In a rented spot,
modeling a plush towel

in the three o'clock light.
No. Face-planted one
pillow over with a nervous

mirror in the corner.
Blushes all over the place
like somebody spilled

the lamp in the corner.
No. Somewhere at another
bowling alley & the pins

break because they can't
handle us. Your hands
flex like accordions

but I thought you played
flute in some small
town's band. Brass body

swelling like an ocean
made out of instruments.
I'm on my knees one

more time, searching
the ceiling for prophets
& reoccurring secrets.

The long song repeats
an old allegory of wrists
& bedposts & a stocking

stretched into transparency.
It's as thin & inelegant
as most of my wants.

DARLING

You didn't need me
& I didn't need you
in the impresario
of scenario wigs
& upbeat whodunits.
No, that's not true
in the land of dress-
up & cuffed outfits.
When we're together
most things overflow
& get backlit: silhouette
of ourselves, collaged
like an octave right
before it concaves
into fabric around
your ankles. What
a mess. We don't need
me & darling, we don't
need you. Outside,
the resistance goes on
for another week. Cops
stay in their bulletproof
vests, lobbing tear gas
for no real reason &
what happens inside
this plywood isolation
needs to mean something.
Yes: we've been at it

since back before
the virus's crescent,
but it's still a selfish
stunt, skipping tonight's
protest. Yes: it's blunt
as sea salt in the sweet
dust where we still
end up undressed
& unrushed no matter
how many sirens holler
at us from out there.

Antagonists All Over

SOMEBODY ELSE SOLD THE WORLD

& eventually the antagonists outdo
themselves by undoing themselves.
Too much time alone motormouthing
under somebody else's big canopy.
Too much familiar anonymity while
their engine smolders with upward
mediocrity. For once, it's as hard
for them as it is for the new Americans,
pedestrians, & art thieves. Almost
everyone is broke & sequestered,
splayed & glazing on rented
sectionals & armchairs. Some
backgrounded by actual masterpieces,
others reframed with posters below
triads of skylights. The originals
& the counterfeits stay in place just
like we do: in great rooms & family
rooms, on mantelpieces topped
by the taxidermy of a glasshouse life.
Mostly see-through, a little smudged,
not inspiring to anybody other than
the thieves & their idle fingers.
I can't even see the stars from down
here in the dance hall glare. Lights
& mirrors abounding & right now
none of us, not even the antagonists
in their splendid lifts, can reach them.

SEE

You're in everything I see
— TYCHO

Backstopped by yellowing leaves, the only thing
I'm thinking about is the congregation of curves
I can't see as you sit on that bench with its mistreated
paint & yellow jackets abounding in sugary light.
Brisk breaths nearby while a jogger huffs autumn
& it sounds like *yes yes*. Somewhere past him:
effigies of my old neglects distanced & waiting
for me to warm my hands over them on nights crisp
with Indiana possibility. I'm no good at choosing
my wants over the fishnet of expectations, but
it's just us in the convocation now. How did I get
lucky like this after my abundance of the other kind
of luck? A dimpled parenthetical & my strings are out
of alignment. Gracious. That smile like an anointment.

LOVE NOTES

It's past midnight & someone's silk shirt
already lost its buttons. The couples hunting
a third are over there near the gallery of mostly

abandoned ideas. No. Yes. When aren't cheap
shots an excuse for quick fantasy? Here we go,

walking past coincidences, nearly holding hands
as if *almost*, too, might be undone in the reverie.
Yes. No. Meanwhile, Miles Davis is Miles

Davis in each & every city of protest, three-
fingering I-told-you-so's in his smirky dialect

of halves & wholes. The bench we finally sit
on is cold & near a river that runs like a tongue
across somebody else's messy unraveling.

THAT FANTASY JOINT

We ain't never going to give
this fucking life up

        —FUTURE

Big-horned parades trumpeting
in my head & the winking flags
over skyscrapers raise their finger Vs
in the new, empty downtown with
boarded windows & spray-paint
idioms. & the brass bands dislocated
by patriotic embouchures—big
tonsils like exclamations, tongues
on point inside the silver-ringed
mouthpieces—now sing songs
of fantasy & prescriptions. Still not
sure when this Percocet extravaganza
became my thing. Sometime after
the window smash & rubber bullets,
sometime after the lockdown
got tagged with homilies of loss.
The humdrum mumble of drugs
& strippers drum the Indy pavement
like litany & apology. But the fingers
on your neck, red toes conundrumed
into whip-smart conversation during
the revolution—that's fantasy ready
to be unfastened like a package
that should have been delivered

on Tuesday. We can't have parties
anymore, but in my fantasy, the band
plays & eyes are made in spotlights.
The next thing you know, we're
our own thing behind cigarette dragons
trying to unzipper, hands like mittens.

LATER ISN'T A TIME

There's still no vaccine, but we can't wait
until later. Around the Soldiers' & Sailors'
Monument, homegrown antagonists watch

from their covered balconies. They check
pocket watches, still ticking from the old
century's windup before sliding glass doors

closed on the litany of naming that starts
every march. The cops hang back, fidgeting
in their gunbelts & eyeing the blonde reporters.

Naming murdered Black people won't stop
rain any more than it stops bullets & not even
shelter-in-place directives relax cop triggers.

Their fingers remain as fat as grease.
Their familiar reactions, hungry as spring
showers. We can't wait: a few miles from here,

Dreasjon Reed ran away from the police
with a T-shirt in one hand & two cell phones
in the other. The cop fired his gun thirteen times.

Then Dreasjon was dying as his phone pointed
upward at sounds: yowling sirens & the cops'
chin-first chatter, his last blue canopy of May.

LOVE NOTES

Again & again until the river next
to where we met becomes a reliquary
of aortic insecurity. Yes. No. All

this vulnerability: on the backbench
in mosquito light, always humming at you

like a bee with foresight. Or just dumb
in the kitchen as the cat bumbles another
jump & keeps trying in the custom of dudes.

The whole circus recedes into circles
of afternoons. The sink, the cat, bottleneck

of your hips. Yes. It's all waiting here,
below a revolving game of skylights. It's all
waiting—unsolvable, our rawhide arabesque.

SOMEBODY ELSE SOLD THE WORLD

When I was a kid,
I watched *Poltergeist*
on a Tuesday & it scared

me so much I was afraid
of the weekday itself.
& still each Tuesday,

the long-fingered trees
outside of my head
are missing some bark.

Antagonists all over,
mostly maskless
as underprepared burglars.

They cough without
covering their tracks.
They leave their shoddy

fingerprints everywhere.
On their self-congratulatory
neighborhood walks,

they acquit their own
nondescript hearts until
they burst & resurrect

inside the TV's particled
white. All voice & hardly
any body. It will be weeks

before anybody cares enough
to change their channel.
In my imagination's spring

forward, the last antagonist
in his foldout throne feels
just like a Black man

for a minute: everyone
crosses the street as soon
as he gets near. His pockets

are turned out to their white
parts. & still, everyone
acts like he sold the world.

WHERE TO BEGIN

X will mark the place
Like the parting of the waves
—RADIOHEAD

I'm trying to get as close to you
as rough-printed fingers get

to guitar strings. Their avuncular
vernaculars fretting just like us.

Their striations, as hard-pressed
& tremulous as us: ampersands,

adagios & allegros, pick fingers
& open hands. Where to begin?

I'm blushing an invitation
to a hibiscus evening. I'm asking

a lot this evening. & promises
before the virus? Everybody made

them with feeling—so many
rib-caged guarantees, half-mooned

with crescent tattoos & heart-
thumping inadequacies. Convex

fingers & long idioms in the habit
of temporary inquiries. My chest

is still cresting inside its loose-
limbed protest. Those leopard print

boots & thighs rising politely—
of course the derelict city outside

is trying to sneak a peek. I can't
wait to lick the rest off of you

with my Midwestern metaphors.
I can't wait to bundle up the back-

in-the-days at the end of a stick
& then: over one shoulder for

a prolonged procession. All of us
getting out of America's slacking

atrium. All of us bopping like
the last platinum jam in the stack.

NOTES

The "Somebody Else Sold the World" cycle is inspired by David Bowie's "The Man Who Sold the World" from *The Man Who Sold the World* (1970).

"On the B Side" is a sing-along with David Bowie's "Rock 'n' Roll Suicide" from *The Rise and Fall of Ziggy Stardust and the Spiders from Mars* (1972).

"Haul" is inspired by the Christian Löffler song of the same name from *Mare* (2016).

"Gymnopédies No. 1," "Gymnopédies No. 2," and "Gymnopédies No. 3" respond to Erik Satie's *Gymnopédies* as perform ed by Pascal Rogé on *Satie: 3 Gymnopédies* (1984).

"Love Notes [Do you love . . .]" is after "Show You the Way" by Thundercat featuring Kenny Loggins and Michael McDonald from *Drunk* (2017).

"HIGHEST" is motivated by "HIGHEST IN THE ROOM" (2019) by Travis Scott.

"Tuesday Feeling" comes from the same-named song on Blood Orange's *Angel's Pulse* (2019).

"Wake Up, Young Lovers" is in response to the Talking Heads' "Swamp" from *Speaking in Tongues* (1983).

"It's All I Have / Daydreaming" is in conversation with Emily Dickinson's poem "It's all I have to bring today (26)" and Radiohead's song "Daydreaming" from *A Moon Shaped Pool* (2016).

"It's Just a Guess" is inspired by Al Green's "Let's Stay Together" from *Let's Stay Together* (1972).

"It's Impossible to Breathe Trees" and "Snakes Because We Say So" are part of a poem cycle activated by Dario Robleto's sculpture *The First Time, the Heart* (2018) in collaboration with *The Virgin Suicides* (1999) by Air.

"Love Notes [Do you love the way . . .]" is after Frank Ocean's "Pink + White" from *Blonde* (2016).

"I Say the Thing for the First Time" is in response to "can't leave without it" by 21 Savage from *i am > i was* (2018).

"Count to Five" is to the melody of Rhye's song of the same name from *Blood* (2018).

"Love Notes [Come through my lit . . .]" is in honor of Prince's "Adore" from *Sign O' the Times* (1987).

"Coincidence/Accident" was inspired by Funkadelic's "Good Thoughts, Bad Thoughts" from *Standing on the Verge of Getting It On* (1974).

"Darling" is in the same octave as Basti Grub's "Darling" (2019).

"See" is in response to Tycho's "See" (featuring Beacon) (2017).

"That Fantasy Joint" is a take on Future's "The Percocet and Stripper Joint" from *DS2* (2015).

"Love Notes [Again & again until . . .]" is a reaction to Lana del Ray's "Summer Bummer" (featuring A$AP Rocky & Playboi Carti) from *Lust for Life* (2017).

"Where to Begin" references Radiohead's "Where I End and You Begin (The Sky Is Falling In)" from *In Rainbows—From the Basement* (2008).

ACKNOWLEDGMENTS

Many thanks to the editors and staffs of the journals in which these poems appeared, sometimes with different titles or in different versions:

Allium: "Coincidence/Accident," "Somebody Else Sold the World [Everything goes better . . .]," "Somebody Else Sold the World [Outside, the antagonists . . .]"

American Poet: "Later Isn't a Time"

The American Poetry Review: "HIGHEST," "Somebody Else Sold the World [& before I knew it . . .]," "Somebody Else Sold the World [& by now even the unemployed . . .]," "Somebody Else Sold the World [I don't know if I . . .]," "Somebody Else Sold the World [When I was a kid . . .]"

Boulevard: "Love Notes [It's past midnight . . .]," "See"

The Chattahoochee Review: "Snakes Because We Say So"

Four Way Review: "Bullet Parts"

Great River Review: "Count to Five," "It's All I Have / Daydreaming," "It's Just a Guess"

The Massachusetts Review: "Tuesday Feeling"

Orion: "It's Impossible to Breathe Trees"

Poetry: "Gymnopédies No. 1," "Gymnopédies No. 2," "Gymnopédies No. 3," "On the B Side" (as "End of Side A")

River Styx: "Haul" (as "Somebody Else Sold the World [I used to live . . .]")

Small Orange: "That Fantasy Joint"

Tin House: "Hearing Damage," "It Was Over Way Back Then" (as "Hearing Damage")

Wildness: "Love Notes [Again & again . . .]," "Love Notes [Do you love . . .]"

"I Say the Thing for the First Time" appeared in the Academy of American Poets Poem-a-Day series on October 2, 2019.

Versions of "Coincidence/Accident," "Let's Get Acquainted," "That Fantasy Joint," and "Where to Begin" appear in the mixed media book *Standing on the Verge & Maggot Brain* (Third Man Books, 2021).

My deepest thanks to the friends and family whose support made these poems possible as the world was breaking apart around us. I miss you all: Erin Belieu, Sherwin Bitsui, Gabrielle Calvocoressi, Oliver de la Paz, Nicholas Galanin, Ross Gay, Terrance Hayes, Richard Johnson, Rodney Jones, A. Van Jordan, Melanie Jordan, Allison Joseph, Ruth Ellen Kocher, Quraysh Ali Lansana, Shara McCallum, Holly McGhee, Marc McKee, Walton Muyumba, Kevin Neireiter, Aimee Nezhukumatathil, Dario Robleto, Cedric Ross, Sean Singer, and Shane Vogel.

I'm grateful to the Academy of American Poets, Indiana Arts Commission, Indiana Humanities, the John Simon Guggenheim Memorial Foundation, the Lannan Foundation, the National Endowment for the Arts, the Rockefeller Foundation Bellagio Center, and United States Artists for their generosity and support.

Thank you to my editor, Paul Slovak, for his trust and insight, and for helping me to figure this project out. I appreciate all you do, man.

Thanks to Kara for helping me through the worst of it. Thanks to Kara for all of it.

Finally, thank you to my mentor and friend Jon Tribble (1962–2019) and to my father, Robert Matejka (1948–2019). I miss you both every day.

POLINA OSHEROV

ADRIAN MATEJKA'S most recent collection of poetry is *Map to the Stars* (Penguin, 2017). His other books are *The Big Smoke* (Penguin, 2013), which was winner of the Anisfield-Wolf Book Award and was a finalist for the National Book Award and Pulitzer Prize; *Mixology* (Penguin, 2009), which was selected for the National Poetry Series; and *The Devil's Garden* (Alice James Books, 2003), winner of the New York/New England Award. Among Matejka's other honors are fellowships from the Academy of American Poets, the Guggenheim Foundation, the Lannan Foundation, the National Endowment for the Arts, the Rockefeller Foundation, and United States Artists. He served as Poet Laureate of the state of Indiana in 2018–19 and lives in Indianapolis, Indiana.

PENGUIN POETS

PENGUIN POETS